To:

From:

Hark! The Herald Angels Sing

BOOK AND CD

VIRGINIA REYNOLDS

PETER PAUPER PRESS INC.
White Plains, New York

—⊗⊗⊗—

All Scripture quotations in this book are taken from the *King James Version* of the Bible, unless otherwise noted. *NKJV* refers to The Holy Bible: *The New King James Version* and *NASB* refers to the *New American Standard Bible*.

With thanks to Liesl Vazquez

Designed by Heather Zschock

See page 61 for information and copyrights on the paintings that appear throughout this book.

Visit us at www.peterpauper.com

Hark! The Herald Angels Sing

Contents

Introduction

⎯⎯⎯⎯⎯⎯

Throughout the ages, angels have graced our lives as symbols of love, kindness, and mercy. The influence of angels reaches far and wide, for they embody the highest ideals to which we aspire. Especially during the holidays, angels bring on their gossamer wings an air of joyful tidings, elegance, and mystery.

The word "angel" derives from the Greek word *angelos* ("messenger"). Sometimes the angel's message is delivered in a song of praise, as retold in the story of the Nativity:

And the angel said unto them, Fear not: for, behold,
I bring you good tidings of great joy, which shall be to all people.
And suddenly there was with the angel a multitude
of the heavenly host praising God, and saying,
Glory to God in the highest,
and on earth peace,
good will toward men.
LUKE 2:10, 13-14

Angels are glittering, glowing, and full of radiance, shining forth with God's illuminating grace. Their brilliance and majesty are awe-inspiring. Because of their dazzling appearance, when angels visit mortals, they must comfort and reassure us as they did the shepherds of Bethlehem, lest we be too overwhelmed to comprehend their important tidings.

Millions of people claim a belief in angels. Whether real or imaginary, angels are so beloved that they have been adopted as part of our year-round lore. Although angels first appeared as religious beings, their influence has spread to the secular sphere as well. Angels now adorn our everyday world, lifting our spirits and warming our hearts.

This book offers a glimpse into the glorious and varied realms in which angels gather both in heaven and on earth. Explore the religious origins and prevalence of angels, angels and love, guardian angels, angels and food, angels in literature and music, and your own angelic self. You will discover facts about angels that amaze and delight. Each chapter combines prose and witty quotes to awaken the angel in you.

So, turn the page and indulge your flights of fancy. And remember, as G. K. Chesterton said, *Angels can fly because they take themselves lightly.*

V. R.

The Origins of Angels

⸰⸰⸰

God created angels to praise Him, serve Him, and carry His messages to the earthly realm. Totally devoid of sin, angels are pure, heavenly creations who act as intermediaries between the divine and human worlds. God gave angels great power, wisdom, and the ability to act—as they often did in the New Testament. When God wanted to announce to Mary that she had been chosen to be Jesus' mother, He sent an angel to deliver the message. Angels appear throughout the Old and New Testaments, as well as the Muslim holy book, the Koran, always performing God's work and sharing God's words.

And, behold, the angel of the Lord came upon him, and a light shined . . .
ACTS 12:7

In the scriptures, encounters with angels are described with great poetry. These meetings, and the messages carried by the angelic messengers, are central to the beliefs of millions of people. The lyrical stories include Jacob's dreams of angels, the protection offered by an angel to Hagar and Ishmael in the desert, and the majestic angels described in the Book of Revelation. Angels cannot be ignored!

The angels are the dispensers and administrators of the Divine beneficence toward us; they regard our safety, undertake our defense, direct our ways, and exercise a constant solicitude that no evil befall us.

JOHN CALVIN

◆

Every visible thing in this world is put in the charge of an angel.

ST. AUGUSTINE

◆

The angel of the Lord encampeth round about them that fear him, and delivereth them.

PSALM 34:7

When a man dies they who survive him ask what property
he has left behind. The angel who bends over the dying
man asks what good deeds he has sent before him.

THE KORAN

◆

The enemy that sowed them is the devil;
the harvest is the end of the world;
and the reapers are the angels.

MATTHEW 13:39

◆

I believe we are free, within limits, and yet there is an unseen hand, a
guiding angel, that somehow, like a submerged propeller, drives us on.

RABINDRANATH TAGORE

The Angelic Hierarchy

———⊖∞∞⊖———

For he shall give his angels charge over thee, to keep thee in all thy ways.

PSALM 91:11

The religious origins of angels trace back to the Bible, where angels served as messengers from God. Later, both Pseudo-Dionysius in *Celestial Hierarchy* and Thomas Aquinas in *Summa Theologica* arranged angels into a hierarchical structure:

RANK	ANGELS	CHARACTERISTICS
First Order	Seraphim, cherubim, thrones	Purity, knowledge, God's messengers
Second Order	Dominations, virtues, powers	Patience, courage, governors of the soul
Third Order	Principalities, archangels, angels	Defenders of religion, human-like qualities

Each level in the hierarchy possesses unique qualities. Scholars have pondered the question of angels in great detail, giving rise to the question, "How many angels can dance on the head of a pin?" The answer is, "As many as want to"!

How many angels are there? Although much ink has been spilled devising mathematical formulas, it is generally believed that God's angelic servants are simply too numerous to count.

A FEW WELL-KNOWN ANGELS . . .

GABRIEL

The *Hero of God* appeared to both the Virgin Mary, to announce the impending birth of Jesus, and to Mohammed. He represents mercy, compassion, and revelation.

RAPHAEL

Raphael is a healer and protector. He is believed to watch over children, travelers, and the sick.

MICHAEL

A powerful warrior angel, protector of the Hebrew people, Michael is also called the *Prince of Light*. He represents decisive action and virtuous judgment.

METATRON

Jewish lore describes Metatron as the guardian of divine wisdom and the most holy of all angels.

URIEL

Called the *Fire of God*, Uriel is associated with illumination and knowledge. The writer Milton suggests that Uriel guards the Tree of Life in the Garden of Eden.

Philosophers are careful to remind us that different people will experience angels in different ways, according to their circumstances or proclivities. Just as our spiritual experiences differ, so too will our encounters with angels.

In all their affliction He was afflicted,
And the angel of His presence saved them;
In His love and in His mercy he redeemed them;
And He lifted them, and carried them all the days of old.

ISAIAH 63:9 NASB

And there appeared an angel unto him from heaven, strengthening him.

LUKE 22:43

◆

For an angel went down at a certain time into the pool and stirred up the water; then whoever stepped in first, after the stirring of the water, was made well of whatever disease he had.

JOHN 5:4 NKJV

◆

Be not forgetful to entertain strangers: for thereby some have entertained angels unawares.

HEBREWS 13:2

The angel Gabriel was sent from
God unto a city of Galilee,
named Nazareth,
To a virgin espoused to a man whose
name was Joseph, of the house of David;
and the virgin's name was Mary.
And the angel came in unto her,
and said, Hail, thou that art highly
favoured, the Lord is with thee:
blessed art thou among women.

LUKE 1:26-28

It is a universal Catholic belief
that not merely every just man,
every child of grace,
but in fact every single
human being here upon earth,
whether Christian or non-Christian,
whether in grace or sin,
remains during its entire life
under the care of a Guardian Angel.

JOSEPH HUSSLEIN

Guardian Angels

W hile all angels are beings of sublime goodness, guardian angels are created especially for our protection. You may not recognize or acknowledge your guardian angel, but this heavenly being watches over, guides, and defends you at all times. As Jean Paul Richter says, *The guardian angels of life sometimes fly so high as to be beyond our sight, but they are always looking down upon us.*

Your guardian angel also soothes and comforts you, and offers you peace of mind in times of crisis. Let your guardian angel's good will enfold you throughout and beyond the holiday season! *And we should pray to the angels, for they are given to us as guardians* (St. Ambrose).

Make yourself familiar with the angels,
and behold them frequently in spirit; for,
without being seen,
they are present with you.
ST. FRANCIS OF SALES

We not only live among men, but there are airy hosts, blessed spectators, sympathetic lookers-on, that see and know and appreciate our thoughts and feelings and acts.

HENRY WARD BEECHER

◆

Each of us has a guardian angel. They're non-threatening, wise, and loving beings. They offer help whether we ask for it or not. But mostly we ignore them.

EILEEN FREEMAN

◆

Therefore for spirits, I am so far from denying their existence that I could easily believe that not only whole Countries, but particular persons, have their Tutelary and Guardian Angels.

THOMAS BROWNE

The Angel Within You

❦

Did you ever hear someone say these magic words, "You're an angel!"? And how many times have you said the same to a friend or helper? You have Scripture on your side! In the Bible, even though most angels or messengers are clearly divine, some are most definitely human. For example, Malachi referred to a priest as a messenger or angel of the Lord (Malachi 2:7), and in the Book of Revelation the elders of the churches of the East were called angels (1:20, 2:1, 2:18).

For every angel fluttering through the skies, there is a divine counterpart here on Earth. Each of us has a golden, celestial self just waiting to be awakened. Every time you lend a helping hand or deliver welcome news, you're acting the part of an angel! Allow the angel within you to emerge in expressions of loving thoughts and kindnesses.

As Rev. Rachel Thompson said in a Christmas Eve sermon: *I am delighted and frightened by the idea of angels, winged messengers of God, blazing with light, burning with God's desire to speak to us. Turning up uninvited and telling us not to be afraid. It doesn't matter whether actual angels (whatever that means, surely not flesh and blood creatures) hovered overhead 2,000 years ago. They exist for us now in the words, the gospels, the songs. They live in our awareness. They live through us.*

If I see one dilemma with Western man,
it's that he can't accept how beautiful he is.
He can't accept that he is pure light, that he's pure love,
that he's pure consciousness, that he's divine.

RAM DASS (RICHARD ALPERT)

Humans are caught in the vortex between the angels on high (our better nature) and the devil down below (our lower or weaker nature). Within great limits, we are able to choose to act on the side of the angels—but it takes a lifetime of attention, care, and commitment to goodness. Let us always truly be on the side of the angels.

Every man hath a good and a bad angel attending
on him in particular all his life long.

ROBERT BURTON

◆

The devil could change. He was once
an angel and may be evolving still.

LAURENCE J. PETER

The question is this: Is man an ape or an angel?
Now, I am on the side of the angels.

BENJAMIN DISRAELI

◆

If a man is not rising upward to
be an angel, depend upon it,
he is sinking downward to be a devil.

SAMUEL TAYLOR COLERIDGE

◆

Men prefer to believe that they are degenerated angels,
rather than elevated apes.

W. WINWOOD ROADE

Angels and Love

———⊰⊱———

We are each of us angels with only one wing. And we can only fly embracing each other.

Luciano de Crescenzo

A long with flowers and hearts, soaring angels have become symbols of love and romance. Cherubs—love angels depicted as chubby, winged babies—were originally multi-bodied beasts, but how they were transformed remains unknown. Cupid, a popular Valentine's cherub, is always portrayed with a bow and arrow. Couples fall in love when pierced by one of his magical arrows. Delight in the dreamy quotes that follow, and surrender yourself to Cupid's charms.

*'Tis strange what a
man may do,
and a woman yet think
him an angel.*

William Makepeace Thackeray

She is as pure, as good, and as beautiful as an angel.

GUY DE MAUPASSANT

◆

The power to love what is purely abstract is given to few.

MARGOT ASQUITH

◆

Love is how you earn your wings.

KAREN GOLDMAN

*Angels and archangels may
have gathered there,
Cherubim and seraphim
thronged the air;
But his mother only,
in her maiden bliss,
Worshipped the beloved
with a kiss.*

CHRISTINA ROSSETTI

• 33 •

Literary Angels

_J_ust as angels abound in religions and religious texts, they also flourish in the world's great secular prose and poetry. Anton Chekhov said: _We shall find peace. We shall hear the angels, we shall see the sky sparkling with diamonds._ Voltaire opined: _It is not known precisely where angels dwell—whether in the air, the void, or the planets. It has not been God's pleasure that we should be informed of their abode._ And, according to John Milton, _Millions of spiritual creatures walk the earth unseen, both when we sleep and when we wake._

Transcend the ordinary and indulge in these further thoughts from a heavenly host of renowned writers:

> _All the Utopias will come to pass_
> _only when we grow wings and all_
> _people are converted into angels._

FËDOR DOSTOEVSKI

It is in rugged crises, in unweariable endurance,
and in aims which put sympathy out of
the question, that the angel is shown.

RALPH WALDO EMERSON

◆

Philosophy will clip
an angel's wings.

JOHN KEATS

◆

The angels laughed.
God looked down from his seventh heaven and smiled.
The angels spread their wings and,
together with Elijah, flew upward into the sky.

ISAAC BASHEVIS SINGER

Angels in Music

———⊗⊗⊗———

Music is well said to be the speech of angels.

THOMAS CARLYLE

A ngels are often depicted as musicians or singers. We are all familiar with images of angelic choirs singing celestial praises and angels blowing mighty trumpets to announce special messages from on high. Included here are the lyrics to some well-loved angelic Christmas songs.

◆

*And flights of angels
sing thee to thy rest!*

WILLIAM SHAKESPEARE,
Hamlet

Hark! The Herald Angels Sing

Hark! the herald angels sing,
Glory to the newborn King;
Peace on earth and mercy mild,
God and sinners reconciled!
Joyful, all ye nations rise,
Join the triumph of the skies;
With th'angelic host proclaim,
Christ is born in Bethlehem!

◆

Refrain
Hark! the herald angels sing,
Glory to the newborn King.

◆

Christ by highest heaven adored;
Christ, the everlasting Lord!
Late in time behold Him come,
Offspring of the virgin's womb.
Veiled in flesh the Godhead see;
Hail th'incarnate Deity,
Pleased as man with man to dwell,
Jesus, our Emmanuel!

◆

Refrain
Hark! the herald angels sing,
Glory to the newborn King.

Angels We Have Heard on High

THIS TRADITIONAL CAROL recalls how shepherds on a long ago winter night were joyously told of the birth of the Christ Child, by angels who appeared to them from on high:

Angels we have heard on high
Sweetly singing o'er the plains,
And the mountains in reply,
Echoing their joyous strains.

Gloria in excelsis Deo,
Gloria in excelsis Deo.

Shepherds, why this jubilee?
Why your joyous strains prolong?
What the gladsome tidings be
Which inspire your heav'nly song?

Gloria in excelsis Deo,
Gloria in excelsis Deo.

Come to Bethlehem and see
Him whose birth the angels sing.
Come adore on bended knee
Christ the Lord, the newborn King.

Gloria in excelsis Deo,
Gloria in excelsis Deo.

It Came Upon the Midnight Clear

It came upon the midnight clear
That glorious song of old,
From angels bending near the earth
To touch their harps of gold.
"Peace on the earth, goodwill to men,
From heav'n's all-gracious King."
The world in solemn stillness lay
To hear the angels sing.

Still through the cloven skies they come
With peaceful wings unfurl'd;
And still their heav'nly music floats
O'er all the weary world.
Above its sad and lowly plains,
They bend on hov'ring wing;
And ever o'er its Babel sounds
The blessed angels sing.

For lo! the days are hast'ning on,
By prophets seen of old,
When with the ever-circling years
Shall come the time foretold.
When the new heav'n and earth shall own
The Prince of Peace, their King,
And the whole of world send back the song
Which now the angels sing.

◆

*I heard a soft melodious voice,
more pure and harmonious than any
I had heard with my ears before;
I believed it was the voice of an
angel who spake to the other angels.*

JOHN WOOLMAN

O Holy Night

O holy night, the stars are brightly shining;
It is the night of the dear Savior's birth.
Long lay the world in sin and error pining,
Till He appeared and the soul felt its worth.
A thrill of hope, the weary soul rejoices,
For yonder breaks a new and glorious morn.
Fall on your knees,
Oh, hear the angel voices!
O night divine, O night when Christ was born!
O night, O holy night, O night divine!

Led by the light of faith serenely beaming,
With glowing hearts by His cradle we stand.
So led by light of a star sweetly gleaming,
Here came the wise men from the Orient land.

The King of Kings lay in a lowly manger,
In all our trials born to be our friend.
He knows our need,
To our weakness no stranger.
Behold your King! before the lowly bend!
Behold your King! your King! before Him bend!

Truly He taught us to love one another;
His law is love and His gospel is peace.
Chains shall He break, for the slave is our brother,
And in His name all oppression shall cease.
Sweet hymns in grateful chorus rise we,
Let all within us praise His holy name.
Christ is the Lord,
Then ever, ever praise we;
His pow'r and glory ever more proclaim,
His pow'r and glory ever more proclaim.

The First Noël

The first Noël, the angel did say,
Was to certain poor shepherds in fields as they lay;
In fields where they lay keeping their sheep,
On a cold winter's night that was so deep.

Refrain
Noël, Noël, Noël, Noël,
Born is the King of Israel.

They looked up and saw a star,
Shining in the East beyond them far;
And to the earth it gave great light,
And so it continued day and night.

Refrain

This star drew nigh to the northwest;
Oe'r Bethlehem it took its rest,
And there it did both stop and stay,
Right oe'r the place where Jesus lay.

Refrain

O Come, All Ye Faithful

O come, all ye faithful,
Joyful and triumphant,
O come ye, O come ye to
    Bethlehem.
Come and behold Him,
    born the King of angels.

Refrain
O come, let us adore Him,
O come, let us adore Him,
O come, let us adore Him,
Christ, the Lord.

Sing, choirs of angels,
Sing in exultation;
Sing all ye citizens of heav'n above:
Glory to God in the Highest.

Refrain

Yea, Lord, we greet Thee,
Born this happy morning;
Jesus, to Thee be glory giv'n;
Word of the Father, now in flesh
    appearing.

Refrain

Adeste fideles,
Laeti triumphantes,
Venite, venite in Bethlehem.
Natum videte, Regem angelorum.
Venite adoremus;
Venite adoremus;
Venite adoremus, Dominum.

Ave Maria

Ave Maria!
gratia plena,
Maria, gratia plena,
Maria, gratia plena,
Ave, Ave. Dominus,
Dominus tecum.
Benedicta tu in mulieribus,
et benedictus,
et benedictus fructus ventris,
ventris tui, Jesus.
Ave Maria!

Ave Maria!
Mater Dei,
Ora pro nobis peccatoribus,
Ora, ora pro nobis
Ora, ora pro nobis peccatoribus,
Nunc, et in hora mortis,
et in hora mortis nostrae,
et in hora mortis, mortis nostrae
et in hora mortis nostrae.
Ave Maria!

What Child Is This?

What Child is this, who laid to rest,
On Mary's lap is sleeping?
Whom angels greet with anthems sweet
While shepherds watch are keeping?

Chorus
This, this is Christ the King,
Whom shepherds guard and angels sing.
Haste, haste to bring Him laud,
The Babe, the Son of Mary.

Why lies He in such mean estate
Where ox and ass are feeding?
Good Christian, fear for sinners here,
The silent Word is pleading.

Chorus
This, this is Christ the King,
Whom shepherds guard and angels sing.
Haste, haste to bring Him laud,
The Babe, the Son of Mary.

So bring Him incense, gold and myrrh;
Come, peasant king, to own Him.
The King of Kings salvation brings;
Let loving hearts enthrone Him.

Chorus
This, this is Christ the King,
Whom shepherds guard and angels sing.
Haste, haste to bring Him laud,
The Babe, the Son of Mary.

Angels from the Realms of Glory

Angels from the realms of glory,
Wing your flight o'er all the earth.
Ye, who sang creation's story,
Now proclaim Messiah's birth.
Come and worship!
Come and worship!
Worship Christ the new-born King!

Shepherds in the field abiding,
Watching o'er your flocks by night.
God with man is now residing,
Yonder shines the infant Light. (*chorus*)

Sages, leave your contemplations,
Brighter visions beam afar.
Seek the great Desire of nations;
Ye have seen his natal star. (*chorus*)

Food for the Angels

When we think of "angelic" foods, our thoughts turn to light, airy confections. With angels involved in so many facets of our lives, it's no wonder we find angelic references even in the foods we eat! Begin with an entrée of angel hair pasta and top it off with a slice of angel food cake for dessert—what could be more heavenly?

◆

Angels are sweet and sour and salty,
wet and dry, hard and soft,
sharp and smooth.
They fly, yes, but in flights
of our own fancy.

F. FORRESTER CHURCH

Angel Hair Pasta with Heavenly Shellfish

◆

2 cans (14-1/2 oz. each) stewed tomatoes

1 can (16 oz.) tomato sauce

2 large cloves garlic, crushed

1-1/2 tsp. Italian seasoning

1 tsp. sugar

Salt and freshly ground pepper to taste

1 lb. shrimp, shelled and deveined

2 dozen mussels, scrubbed

2 dozen Little Neck clams, rinsed

1 lb. angel hair pasta, cooked and drained

Freshly grated Parmesan cheese to serve

Freshly chopped parsley to garnish

Place stewed tomatoes, tomato sauce, garlic, Italian seasoning, sugar, salt, and pepper in a large saucepan. Stir well, bring to a boil, reduce heat, and simmer 5 minutes. Add shrimp, mussels, and clams. Cover and simmer just until mussels and clams open. Discard any that don't open. Place cooked angel hair in a large serving bowl. Spoon sauce and shellfish over and toss gently. Sprinkle with Parmesan cheese and garnish with parsley. Serve immediately.

6 servings

◆

Man did eat angels' food:
he sent them meat to the full.

PSALM 78:25

Angel Food Cake

◆

1 cup sifted cake flour
1-1/4 cups sugar, divided
10 egg whites
1 tsp. cream of tartar
1/4 tsp. salt
1 tsp. vanilla extract
1/4 tsp. almond extract

Preheat oven to 350°. Sift flour 3 times with 1/2 cup sugar. Beat egg whites until foamy. Add cream of tartar and salt, and beat until stiff but not dry. Whip in remaining sugar, 2 tablespoons at a time. Add vanilla and almond extract. Sift about 1/4 cup of flour and sugar mixture at a time over the batter and fold in until no flour shows. Turn into an ungreased 10-inch tube pan and bake for 45 minutes. Invert pan on neck of a bottle or funnel and let cake cool thoroughly in pan.

Modern-Day Angels

Everyone entrusted with a mission is an angel . . .
All forces that reside in the body are angels.

MOSES MAIMONIDES

*P*eople acting in their communities can be angels in the best human sense. Financial backers of a Broadway show are often referred to as "angels," because they make things happen. We too can be angels by making things happen through acts of goodness to families, friends, strangers, and the needy. We can help build community in our neighborhoods, schools, professional and civic associations, and towns and cities. We can be messengers (angels) of a saner, more peaceful world.

Those of us who serve homeless people a nourishing meal at Thanksgiving, deliver meals to needy elderly through Meals on Wheels, bring our communities together for a First Night or other celebration, speak out against injustice—we are all angels too.

We all have our angelic impulses and our angelic moments. Being a real angel, however is a full-time job!

I'm in love with a God who sends his brilliant angel messenger
not to the king's palace or to the high priest, but to shepherds.
The poorest of the working poor, guarding the wealth,
the livestock, of others. Almost outcast, but tethered by
a thread of responsibility to the community.

REV, RACHEL THOMPSON

◆

With a little reason and much heart,
we can change many things,
or move mountains.

ALBERT SCHWEITZER

◆

We have heard the angels from on high. Let us also hearken to the angels within, from whose bidding we would seek peace on earth, good will to men.

Art Credits

Jacket, cover, and p. 32:
Schadow, Wilhelm (1788-1862),
Mignon
(Museum der Bildenden Kuenste,
Leipzig, Germany).
© Scala/Art Resource, NY

p. 8: Raphael (1483-1520),
Coronation of the Virgin: detail of musical angels
(Pinacoteca/Vatican Museums, Vatican State).
© Scala/Art Resource, NY

pp. 12 and 52: Memling, Hans (1425/40-1494),
Angels making music
(Koninklijk Museum, Antwerp, Belgium).
© Scala/Art Resource, NY

p. 16: Campin, Robert (c.1375-1444),
Angels. Detail from the Nativity,
Adoration of the Shepherds
(Musée des Beaux-Arts, Dijon, France).
© Scala/Art Resource, NY

p. 25: Saraceni, Carlo (1585-1620),
Saint Cecilia
(Galleria Nazionale d'Arte Antica, Rome, Italy).
© Scala/Art Resource, NY

p. 29: Rosso Fiorentino (1494-1540),
Music-making Angel
(Uffizi, Florence, Italy).
© Scala/Art Resource, NY

p. 37: Matteo di Giovanni di Bartolo (c.1430-1495),
Saint Barbara enthroned among angels and saints.
Detail
(S. Domenico, Siena, Italy).
© Scala/Art Resource, NY

p. 40: Raphael (1483-1520),
Poetry. Detail from the ceiling of the
Stanza della Segnatura
(Stanze di Raffaello, Vatican Palace, Vatican State).
© Scala/Art Resource, NY

p. 47: Reni, Guido (1575-1642),
An Angel
(Palazzo Vecchio, Florence, Italy).
© Scala/Art Resource, NY

p. 56: Melozzo da Forli (1438-1494),
Music-making Angel
(Museo del Prado, Madrid, Spain).
© Scala/Art Resource, NY